To Frank—
a fine Poet
and a great
voice.
—Doug

THE MAN IN THE BOOTH
IN THE MIDTOWN TUNNEL

BY DOUG HOLDER

ČERVENÁ BARVA
PRESS

Čevená Barva Press
P.O. Box 440357
W. Somerville, MA 02144-3222

www.cervenabarvapress.com

Bookstore: www.thelostbookshelf.com

ISBN: 978-1-4357-1957-6

Library of Congress Control Number: 2008931279

Cover Photo: Library of Congress, Prints and Photographs Division, Historic American Buildings Survey or Historic American Engineering Record, Reproduction Number "HAER NY, 31-NEYO, 166-28"

Cover Design: William J. Kelle

Design: Steve Glines

Text is set in Albertus MT 12 pt.
Titles are set in Auriol 14 pt.

ACKNOWLEDGEMENTS

Grateful acknowledgement to the following magazines in which these poems appeared:

Presa, Gloomy Cupboard, Lyrical Somerville (The Somerville News), *Writer's Journal, Wolfhead Quarterly, PLAZM, Voices Israel, 96inc., Poetry.About.Com, Armchair Aesthete, Spare Change News, Butcher Block, Mothwing.com, The Boston Poet, City of Poets: 18 Boston Voices* (Anthology), *Healing Times, The Harvard Mosaic* (Harvard University), *First Class, Out of the Blue Writers Unite* (Anthology), *Senior Times, Crooked River, COMPOST, Fenway News, and Poesy.*

I want to thank Gloria Mindock and William J. Kelle of the Červená Barva Press for their unwavering support of my work. I also want to thank Richard Wilhelm for his help editing this collection. And as always thanks to my wife Dianne Robitaille and her critical eye, not to mention Steve Glines and all those wonderful "Bagel Bards" who meet every Saturday morning in my hometown of Somerville, Massachusetts.

Contents

INTRODUCTION

I was a participant in a poetry reading for the Čevená Barva Press in Cambridge, MA in the early spring of 2008. After the reading, one of the participating poets Elaine Terranova said that my work reminded her of Edgar Lee Masters' "*Spoon River Anthology*." The "*Spoon River Anthology*" (1915) is a collection of unusual, short, free form poems that describes the life of a fictional small town "Spoon River." The collection includes hundreds of portraits of the denizens of the town, their lives and losses.

From our conversation, I realized that a generous share of my poetry has been character-study. From portraits of myself, my family, people I met at my job on the psychiatric ward at McLean Hospital (where I have worked for many years), and all the characters I have talked to, (and more often than not observed) in Cambridge, Boston, and Somerville for decades, my work has been defined by the study of people.

I don't live in a provincial burg like Masters' characters do, but in my small niche, in my corner of Somerville, at my usual seat in the Sherman Café in the Union Square section of the city, I have written about all the many named and nameless faces that have been a source of fascination for me my whole life.

–Doug Holder

THE MAN IN THE BOOTH
IN THE MIDTOWN TUNNEL

THE MAN IN THE BOOTH IN THE MIDTOWN TUNNEL

* As a kid I always wondered about the man in the small booth in the middle of the Midtown Tunnel; the tunnel in NYC that goes from the borough of Queens to Manhattan.

The cars stream
Under a frozen
Catatonic
East River.
And the man
In the booth
Paces the perimeter
Of his cage.

He fumes
With the fumes.
And feels
The river's pressure
Above his head.
And he has
Lost his face
Long ago
In a blue uniform.

And the sun
And the fresh air,
Merely a hint.

And we are

...

Faceless and a blur,
Behind thick plates
Of light-bleached glass.
And we will
All remain
Ignorant of
Each other.

And there is
No light
At the
End of
The Midtown
Tunnel.

THE WOMAN WHO SAT ON THE TOILET FOR TWO YEARS

* The Boston Globe. March 13, 2008.

(Wichita, Kansas) Authorities are considering charges in the bizarre case of a woman who police said sat on her boyfriend's toilet for two years.

And when you
Think of it
It is only a hassle
To get up from
What you revisit
Time and time
Again.

All that you
Take in, in
This life
Is a wash
Anyway.

All your slick
Posturing.
The endless histrionics
Wind up
In a dance
Cheek to cheek
Above the bowl.

All your
Upstream paddling
Leads to those
Placid waters.
And royalty
Yes
Even a king
Will make his
Royal flush.

DAVIS SQUARE, SOMERVILLE: COLONIAL WOMAN AT THE AU BON PAIN.

* I used to see a woman dressed in colonial garb stop on her way to work at the Au Bon Pain Café.

Such a prim contrast
To all these bejeweled
Belly buttons
And the tight
Grip of
Spandex pants...

My lady of the past.

Oh yes...
A contradiction
As she slips
A cell phone
In her billowing
Antique dress.

My lady of the past.

And underneath
A bone-white bonnet
Lies the waves and crests
Of luxuriant
Beguiling
Purple hair.

My lady of the past.

I expected a carriage
To whisk her away
But she primly
lifts her laced hem
To meet the screech
Of the subway.

BOOK SEDUCER

You have revealed
Your subtext to me
In a hushed
Intimate encounter.

I seduced you
On a train.
Lovingly
Folding your
Pages
With dog ears,
Highlighting what
I loved about you
With deep
heart-red ink.

And even now,
I talk you up
With people
I meet,
Yet I abandoned you
On some commuter
Rail seat.

THE FAMILY PICTURE

It has the smell of
Decomposition.
Dog-eared
Curled
Sepia-tinted
Fringes.
A moth-eaten family
Rigidly positioned-
A hierarchy of rows.

Perhaps a maiden aunt
Her face
A dour, down turned affair
Relegated to the back.

And the two boys—
One looks defiantly at the camera
While the other
Ponders the ground.

Their vision
Already in a cast
All framed with barren winter branches
Nothing will last.

TRAINING HER PET

She kept a tight
Leash on him.
Pulling Harder
When he strayed.

They walked through
The park
With the same, clipped
Brisk gait,
Their eyes squarely
On the well-worn path.

Coming home
To the tasteful,
Well-appointed living room—

And he knew his place,
Scurrying to his usual corner.

She knew then
That they would be
Ready to marry
Soon.

PRIVATE DINING UNDER A BLOUSE

*For my nephew Josh.

In the middle of our conversation
And the din
Of the large dining room
She lifted her blouse
Her baby blindly
Grabbing her nipple
With his mouth,
The blouse covered him
Like a shroud
For private dining.

I saw
The infant emerge
Sleeping
Held in an untroubled
Dream.

I sucked on my straw
Flattening the plastic stem
Still awake
And troubled.

SEDUCTION

* Based on a conversation I had with a veteran poet in a local bar.

So often
She entered his room
After berating his father—
A man sacked
In a beaten chair
Living in a defeated
Rumpled shirt.

And once again
She presents herself
With a black negligee
At the cusp of his bedroom door,
Like a seductive
Maternal whore.

And he argued with himself...
Trying not to believe
In that horrific vision
At his door

But still...
He needed--
He wanted her,
More and
More.

I SAW MYSELF ON THE DUDLEY BUS THAT DAY

I saw myself on the Dudley bus that day
The eyes: a blinking, flirt
With the mid-winter's sun—
Watching
The slow, fade
Of a dying afternoon,
His face shadowed
In five o'clock.

Half-light,
No hair.
A bus of exiles
Each mired
In their personal
Affairs.

And that man,
Perhaps me?
Looked a million
Miles away.

I believe I saw
Him briefly yesterday
And for a first time
On that day
We saw each other
And quickly
Turned away.

IN THE TWIN TOWERS

* My take on a murder that took place in the Cambridge, Mass. projects
some years ago

In the Twin Towers
Sequestered from the immediate below
An elderly couple
Soaked in their own tepid sweat
From the oppressive breath of project heat
For a moment tried to remember
The vague idea of themselves
That propelled them
Thirty years ago.

He can hear from the living room
That antique bell chime—
He has turned into a herniated butler.

She rings again
How delicate, demure, genteel.

He thinks of her gnarled hands
The liver spots—
Musing how her ring held on
To the bony corpse of her finger.

Entering her room
He smiles
"I have nothing to say to you," she says.
As if it was necessary.

Her skin
As lifeless,
Bloodless
As the diluted
Tea she drinks.

He puts his arms around her
How strange this sudden passion
She arouses in him.

How he missed her cries
Her bones snapping in such an
Easy sequence
The heat rising furiously
Up the vents
It would soon be unbearable.

KILLING TIME AT THE 99

* A bar, like many bars, in Cambridge, Mass.

A skeletal man
His torso
Barely supports
A crisp white shirt—
His forehead
Violated by a jet black
Wedge of his toupee—

And a businessman's
Perfunctory
Flirtation
With the scripted chatter
Of the barmaid.

(she assures us a few times
it is not the heat
but the humidity
that bothers her—)

He looks
To his
Audience
Staring into
The icy abyss
Of his frosted glass.

An old man
Pipes up
And fawns over
A prized cat
Who I think
With such
Suffocating attention
Must be miserable,
And I drink
To all
This loneliness
Made visible.

AN OLD HARVARD MAN

And there you were
Dumfounded.
Walking the ward
After angrily spraying
The statue of John Harvard
A crimson red.
The Japanese tourists
Snapping your picture
As if you were
Part of the attraction.

Carted away
From the scene.
A yearly performance
Of a fifty year old
Sweating
In a soiled tweed jacket
Smiling sheepishly,
The rotting stumps of teeth
An omen
Of your insides.

Still,
You demand an explanation
For your expulsion
From these,
Effete ivied walls,
And wait to register
Again,
In the spring.

POSTAL WORKER

The supervisor
Counts the seconds
As you wipe
The crumbs from your
Face and return
To your post.

Your hands
Anonymous
Callused, pedestrian
You feed
A rapid,
Stream of letters
To a ravenous federal machine.

Your eyes dimmed
For years
From the sea of manila
The bland white face
Of the mail
Faces scarred
With zips.

You feel
Ready to
Be returned to
Your sender.

RICHARD III IN HOLYWOOD

Richard
You are not over the hump—
The Armani suit
Fits as tightly as a glove
Highlighting your deformity—
A tumor
That stretches the expensive fiber.

Varicose veins cover you
Like a road map
Save the whites of
Your dimmed eyes.

On your walk
Along the strip
Of your diminished kingdom
The lads on the corner
Whisper,
"Who's the gimp?"

The lady in the bar
Rejecting your insidious advances
With an air of cultivation:
"Get lost, you ill-formed toad."

The ghosts that haunt you
Vanished
Now that you
Popped the Prozac.

Yet…
In confidence
You tell me-
Your singular audience
That you have deals to cut
Evil to consummate
During your
Highly rated
Winter of discontent.

And I answer, intrigued:
"Hey—
Let's do lunch"

THE LOVE LIFE OF J. EDGAR HOOVER

The breeze crumples
Your sheer caftan
Mother downstairs
Off her rocker
Your loyal assistant
Straddles you
And in your ecstasy
Your bulldog face
Creased in effeminate screams
Reveling
With your agent's
Successful probe
Deeper and deeper
Into your stagnant well.

Reamed,
Cleaned
You sleep
With his
Gentle kiss.

SHEA STADIUM: 1972

The smell of cigar smoke
Reminded me...
Old men gripping scorecards
The Woodside train
A blur on
The tracks to Flushing.

The concession stand
Pucks of hamburgers
Emerging from a sea
Of grease and onions.

I sat high
In the bleachers,
Still
Listening for the
Hard slap
Of Seaver's fastball,
Sneaking down to
The depths
For the boxes
And a diamond
Glittering
In a hot
Summer's sun.

Gawky and shambling...
But here
I was an Adonis
Of batting averages,
Strikeouts, stats.

Here I was
Graceful, smooth
As an athlete...

...

Nine innings--
Played out
With rules,
Final resolutions,
Perhaps
Poetic justice.

And as Agee
Circled the bases
In an arrogant
Homerun strut
I wondered
If my
Life would
Ever be
So
Clear cut.

FOR SARAH

* For my niece Sarah Holder

And she ran.
Legs—
Almost lifting her
Into flight.
Eyes--
Radiant
With wonder
Not an inkling
Of her
Abrupt slide—

Her joyous romp
Suddenly terminated—
Flat
On her backside
And even in her father's
Arms she cried.

She could never run that way again--
No matter how she tried.

CAMBRIDGE, MASS: TWO OLD WOMEN

Two old women
Walk down
My street
Each morning.

Lugging two
Shopping bags
And two widow's humps.

Arm in arm
A tight embrace
Of frail appendages
Pushing each other
At no more
Than a snail's pace.

Each morning
Refusing the pull
Of age's inertia

A daily ritual
Of decrepit defiance
Walking the ground
That will own them.

TO BE SEEN

Please.
See me.
My ponytail
Wagging behind
My accountant face.

Watch me.
Manipulate
The small bits
Of green food
Like decorative pieces
Of a puzzle
Lying on
A huge
White plate.

See me.
I am branded.
With leather
Tattoos
Cutting-edge
Leather shoes.

Rings pierce my nipple and nostril
They dance
On my flapping tongue
Who says we waste
Being young?

...

Look.
There is a tuft
Of fuzz
Hanging limply
From my weak chin.

So ignore them,
Hear my silent
Din.

DIANNE AT SLEEP

* For my wife Dianne

As she lays
Framed pictures
Splashes of muted
Color arise
From her
Tousled head.

In her sleep
She mutters
Some B
Movie script
From her
Nightly play,
While the
Cat consumes her
With his
Green eyes
A hungry
Verdant blaze.

We both lay
Just below
Her breasts
And sleep
In a lap
For transient
Treasured
Guests.

MT. AUBURN HOSPITAL: 11 TO 7 SHIFT.

The hospital room.
A hunched
Wizened old man.
The bloody stool
Of the commode.

I turned the lights off.
In the pitch black
He yelled:
"Help, Me! Help, Me!, Help Me!"

I switched the light on.
He smiled,
Nodding assurances
His cloudy eyes
Almost sparkling
With his smile.
"I'm going back to work, you know."

Again
The commode
Raises its
Red flag
And his
Bones seem
To push
Through
His skin.

"Married 50 years,
longer than you
have been alive."

He gave me an
Elfin chuckle.

I turned the
Light off
The black engulfed
Us.

YOUNG POET

* A Reading at Stone Soup at T.T The Bears, in Cambridge, Mass. some years ago.

She illuminated
The dark bar
Like the distant
Pristine light
From the maw
Of a cave.

Her expression
Dramatic
Practiced
But every so often
Betraying herself
With a nervous tic
A flutter of the lid
An awkward positioning
Of her legs.

She talked
Of making love,
As if a new discovery.
How he fills
Her remote crevices
She is he
He is she.

The amorous
Couplings
Small rooms
Cambridge Victorians
Cigarette smoke
Ash

Lipstick traces
Romantic places
Half empty glasses
On the bed stand
The lingering scent
Remembered phrases...

Looking at her audience
Her body willowy
Fluid
Not yet marked.
Her face impervious
To the revealing
Glare of the spotlight
Her hair
Draping down her shoulders
Looking
Like it was
Glazed with honey.

From
The back
In the corner
An old woman
Lifted her head
From the rim of a shot glass
And cackled
Breaking the spell:
"What's the big deal kid,
any two dogs can do that."

SIG KLEIN'S FAT MAN'S SHOP

The sign
A flashing
Fat man
Clad only
In expansive
Underwear
Loomed outside
A rooming house window
Like a shut-in's
Desperate move
Of self-exposure.
Comforting us
With the notion
That there is indeed
"A fit for any sized man,"
Just look
What's underneath.

HIS LAST IMPACT ON THE METROPOLIS

* Based on The Boston Globe account of a man who passed away on the
Red Line.

When he passed
It was on the subway
The Daily dropped
From his hands.
His head
Gave up its life-long
Struggle with gravity.
He dropped
Like some flimsy theatrical prop.
A middle-aged man
His swan song
The indignity of
A comic roll on the floor—
The subway's screeching halt,
The trains backed up
From Cambridge to Dorchester.
Bulky, twisting
Metal snakes.

The processional
With passengers
On either
Side of the stretcher
Watching some forgotten
Ineffectual man
Make his mark
Freezing the rush hour
Stopping them
Dead
In their
Tracks.

HOME

Oh the frustration!
Rubbing your hands
Red and raw.
Wondering if the spots
Are flecks
Or the rude stain
Of ingrained dirt,
As you run
The sweeper
Over the same
Blue-carpeted square
Dust still settles
In the wake
Of your effort.
The cat's hair
Drapes itself
On the upholstery
Like a thread-bare gown.

Damn!
The light
Never falls
The way you want it.
You have cleaned
The windows,
Arranged the blinds,
But it streaks through
Untamed
Such brazen energy.

No matter—
You must scrub the floor
Raw.

Something is bound
To leave its mark.

THE LIFE OF THE PARTY

Even the sparkling wine
Seemed to wink
Seductively at you.

After all,
You were
The center
The words
Fell like pearls
From your mouth.

The approving smiles
From the women
The perfect opiate
Delightful
But never enough.

And for this moment
You were a man
Among the men
Above--
Out of reach
From the subtext
Of their threats.
You weaved
Through the crowd
Like some predatory cat.

And then
In the bathroom mirror
Who was this impostor
Short and bald
Struggling with
His fly
His eyes red-rimmed
And bulging
Staring at you
In a comic assault
With your pants down.

You now
Remembered your place.

MOTHER AND DAUGHTER

In the living room
Her mother
A solid mound,
Dormant
Her girth
Spilling
Over the easy
Chair,
Hypnotized by the
TV screen
Frozen on a Jeopardy
Question.

And what a chore
It will be
To move mother.
To escape
The decades long
Anchor of the
Living room.

How many barbs
The sinister, humorous
Exchanges
The race for the
Upper hand
The life-long
Symbiosis
Riding on each other's
Stooped back.

A monumental task...
"And who is the victim?
You ask.

A DREAM OF MINNIE BAUM

* For my late grandmother, Minnie.

I sit in the deep creases of her sundress,
A purple flourish of fabric flowers,
Stunned by the musty cabal of her perfume.
My head resting on her soft deflated breasts
She exchanges Yiddish for English with mother
Tit for tat.

I am trapped...
My stomach leaden with chicken fat.
Bronx cheers from the pavement below
I'm in familial ground
Nesting in the lap
Of a long dead grandmother
With my mother's
Jealous eyes
Fixed on me.

THE LAST HOTDOG

* For Sy Baum

Long after he was hungry—
It was the last thing
He asked for
With any appetite.

She brought it
To his sick bed,
He bit through
The red casing
The familiar orgasm
Of juice
Hitting the roof
Of his mouth
In some facsimile
Of his youth.

Bites of memory:
The summer ballparks
The steam rising
From the carts
In warm, fragrant clouds
Against the shock
Of early spring cold.

The mysterious, darkened
Delicatessens
Under the elevated tracks.
The Bronx gray afternoons
Dining with his father
The sullen
Colorless meals
Though the franks
Fully garnished
The bright
Yellow and green
Of mustard
And relish.
He swallowed hard
It was all
Too much
To digest.

WATCHING HER READ MY POEM

Did I detect a smile
At the corner of her mouth?
She did hover on my page
A bit more than the others...

Obviously intelligent—
A creased noble brow
In the midst of an exegesis
Folding the paper
For an exclusive focus on mine—
Then standing
Her proud purposeful gait
To the bus's door
Then on to the street
And with perfect aim
Right into
the trash.

LOST GIRL ON THE PSYCHIATRIC WARD

Standing in the middle of the ward
A thin scrim of sweat
Glistens on her nascent mustache
Apologizing to the thin air
Her hands on her hips—
Disgust for the phantoms.

She is on guard
For the vulpine machinations
Of the silent, incessant voices
Chattering in her cortex
A murderous Greek Chorus
Slapping at the hollows
Of her skull.

BOSTON: SCREAMING DOWN NEWBURY STREET

Surprising.
She was
So well coiffed.
Weaving, streaking
With a horrified scream
Past the coolly
Posturing mannequins
Their upturned noses
Dripping sweat
From nostril rings.

Sitting in cafes
From beneath their contempt—
They watched her
Frantic strides
Wondering where
She bought
Her pumps.

AUTHORIAL BUSTS: BATES ROOM. BOSTON PUBLIC LIBRARY.

Expression
Frozen
Ancient poses.
Their stern brows
Creased in
Eternal concentration.
Their torsos-
Ephemeral, dust.

These mute
Talking heads.
So many
Silent demands.
Lining the walls
Points of statuesque light
A confluence of past
And present.

They are backed
By the brittle spines
Of time- worn,
leather bound
tomes.

To whom do these
Ossified men
Address?
What do they
Seem to defend
Against?

...

The patrons in
Fetal curls,
Around their books.
Dime Store half glasses askew?

Some lurking sacrilege?
A looming defilement?

They guard
Some archaic sensibility
They have no head
For anything else.

AN OLD BRAHMIN DESCENDING

* An observed scene on Bay State Rd. in Boston

Grab the black hand of the attendant.
The one you avoided so long
In your rarefied cocoon.
Your fur coat
Will no longer distance you
As you shiver
From the chill
Of an eighty degree day.

Down the Brownstone's steps
Squinting
In this alien spring light
You wonder:
"Where are the Dutch Elms?"

Their shady gentility
Cut from the scene
Like some unruly cancer.
And those college students!
Preening on the grass
Like young animals.

Your face is a comical mask of chalk white.,
A stranger to the sun and yourself.

On such a warm day
A cold shock of comprehension
You are long past due.

HEROIN

To think
How his body
Shed its ulcerated skin
Rested near the maw of death
Sunning at the brink of the abyss.
Then to die
In the midst
Of bliss.

CIGARETTE ON THE PSYCHIATRIC WARD

"Can I have a light?'

What was that sudden spark in her eyes?
That flame
From cloudy, dormant pupils,
When I lit her cigarette.

The sudden driving ambition
To inhale
The sunken chest's almost boastful expansion.
The smoke filling the yawning cavity.
A woman of substance...

Until she exhaled.

PAY PHONES ON THE BOSTON COMMON

A bank of payphones
Like a historical monument
On the Common.

No men clutching receivers
Looking around fearfully
Watching their backs
For the friends of "Eddie Coyle."

We are wireless
We won't be domestic abusers
Slamming our fist against
The box's cold metal face
Demanding change.

The cells
Now flick open
In a personal
Fuck you
To you.

But I still
Hold your large
Ungainly mouthpiece
Bleed my hot breath
Into you
and pull
the hard plastic line
hoping
there is
still
someone
out there.

MOVIE MARQUEE

An ordinary man
A step up
On a ladder
Bathed in light
Now a man of letters-
Placing each
With care
Exacting precision
For he is a man with a title.
Still—
He is no movie star
Yet
He is part
Of the coming
Attraction.

RAT'S CARCASS

A deep blue sky
A sun bright
With its twelve o'clock high,
Summer with its largess
Why must it be spoiled
By that dead rat's carcass?

Why,
When the long legs of ladies
Pass in a tanned revue
Does that rat's carcass
Cruelly
Come into view?

With my flesh so supple
My robust health not subtle
Why must I see the rat's carcass,
What seems to be the trouble?

A TROPHY WIFE

Yes,
It is a shame.
Her appearance
That is...

But she
Still casts
Well
In the proper light
That is
There is no doubt
That she is a haunting
Elegant figure.

I wonder
Is there a certain
Symmetry
To our
Distant polarities?

Yes...
Her youth
Is wasted on her
All that unearned
Attention
The worship
The hypnotic stares
That she is
In receipt of.

I've never been so proud of myself.

LONGING: FOR WHAT?

You felt
It press
Again
In your
Stomach
The churning
Guttural groans
In the
Dead of
Night.

It really
Has never
Revealed itself
Always a phantom
Gnawing...
Demanding that
Its hungry
Void be filled,
But with what?

And you—
With such
Adult concerns
Negotiating the daily
Press of the flesh
Meeting the growing demands
Dodging the barbs
Of every day...

And at night
It is all
You can do
Not to rip
The nipple
From your complacent
Baby's mouth
"She must be weaned." you think.

And then
You cry
Yet again
Over spilled milk.

"NO IRON SPIKE CAN PIERCE A HUMAN HEART AS ICILY AS A PERIOD IN THE RIGHT PLACE." (ISAAC BABEL)

In the end
It is the period.
It is the terminus
Of the last word
The last utterance
Heard.

It breaks the back
Of the most
Impassioned flourish
With a punctuated hush.

On the page
And on the stage
The plot may thicken
And then climax
But in the orchestra pit
They always play the final taps.

And that's the last
We will ever hear of
It, him, or her

Period.

FIRST NIGHT ON THE JOB ON THE PSYCH. WARD

* McLean Hospital. 1982.

The night seemed perfectly cast
Stormy, thunder, and rain
The patient was biblical
Long hair and a beard,
With his staff
At his command.

He put a paternal hand on me,
And called me his finest creation.

What could I do but thank him?
He smiled
With divine patronization
Undoubtedly I was a
Much-valued acolyte.

Then suddenly
A flash from the storm
Lit the building
In a momentary
Spectral glow.
A clap of thunder
Howled down
The locked ward.

He looked at me
Like a proud teacher,
Patting me on the back
"Good work kid, good work."

AT THE FRUIT STAND

* Outside the old Woolworth's Building, Washington St., Boston, Mass.

"Flip her the bird," he told the young man,
with the green assertion of a cigar
clenched between his stained teeth.

The boy held the melon
Like he was cupping a breast
His hands in fluid movement
Through the wet jungle of grapes,
His fingers emerging glistening
From the exploration.

"She thinks she's a class act."
He clenched harder on the cigar
Halting the smoke's circulation
A limp appendage
Hanging from his brown mouth…
"Dump her."

The boy packed the bananas,
Letting his hands
Slide down the yellow
Unblemished skin,
Wanting to peel it—
To have its fruit
In his mouth.

"I'll give her
another call.

Biography

Doug Holder's poetry and prose has appeared in *The Boston Globe Magazine, Rattle, Café Review, the new renaissance, Poesy, Home Planet News, Main Street Rag, Caesura, Quercus Review, Illyia's Honey, Istanbul Literary Review, Dudley Review* (Harvard University), *Sahara, Northeast Corridor* and many others. Holder's audio and videotaped interviews with contemporary poets are archived at Harvard, and Buffalo University libraries as well as Poet's House in New York City. Holder is the founder of the *Ibbetson Street Press* of Somerville, Mass., the cofounder of the Somerville News Writers Festival, the curator of the Newton Free Library Poetry Series, book review editor of the *Wilderness House Literary Review,* the arts editor for *The Somerville News,* and the Boston editor for *Poesy.* He recently was a guest of the Voices Israel literary organization and conducted workshops and read from his work in Jerusalem, Tel Aviv and Haifa.

His two most recent collections of poetry are *No One Dies at the Au Bon Pain,* (sunnyoutside), and *Of All The Meals I Had Before,* (Červená Barva Press). He holds an M.A. in English and American Literature and Language from Harvard University.